WITHDRAWN

Our Nation's Pride

The United States Flag

By Amanda Doering Tourville
Illustrated by Todd Ouren

Content Consultant:
Richard Jensen, Ph.D.
Author, Scholar, and Historian

Magic Wagon

Visit us at www.abdopublishing.com

Published by Magic Wagon, a division of the ABDO Publishing Group, 8000 West 78th Street, Edina, Minnesota, 55439. Copyright © 2008 by Abdo Consulting Group, Inc. International copyrights reserved in all countries. All rights reserved. No part of this book may be reproduced in any form without written permission from the publisher. Looking Glass Library™ is a trademark and logo of Magic Wagon.

Printed in the United States.

Text by Amanda Doering Tourville
Illustrations by Todd Ouren
Edited by Patricia Stockland
Interior layout and design by Nicole Brecke
Cover design by Nicole Brecke

Library of Congress Cataloging-in-Publication Data
Doering Tourville, Amanda, 1980-
  The United States flag / Amanda Doering Tourville ; illustrated by Todd Ouren ; content consultant, Richard Jensen.
     p. cm. — (Our nation's pride)
  Includes bibliographical references and index.
  ISBN 978-1-60270-116-8
  1. Flags—United States—Juvenile literature. 2. Flags—United States—Pictorial works—Juvenile literature. I. Ouren, Todd. II. Jensen, Richard J. III. Title.
CR113.D64 2008
929.9'20973—dc22
                          2007034072

Table of Contents

Our Country's Flag

A flag flies high in front of your school. Its red-and-white stripes move gently in the breeze. Its white stars show bright against their blue background. This is the United States Flag.

How did the flag become the nation's most important symbol? The flag has a long history. It begins with the birth of the United States of America.

Fighting for Freedom

In the 1700s, America was made up of 13 colonies. Great Britain ruled the American colonies. Many Americans felt that Great Britain was treating them unfairly. America went to war with Great Britain to gain its freedom.

During the war, soldiers carried different flags.

Each ship had its own flag. Some flags looked

too much like the British flag.

Having so many different flags was confusing.

So in 1777, lawmakers decided that the new nation

needed one flag.

The First Flag

Most people believe that Betsy Ross designed the first flag. The first flag had 13 stripes. The stripes were red and white. The flag had 13 white stars on a blue background.

The 13 stripes and the 13 stars were symbols of the original 13 states. These states formed the new United States of America.

Lawmakers did not say what shape the flag should be. They did not say where the 13 stars should be placed on the blue background either. So, flags were made in different shapes and sizes.

Flag makers placed the stars differently. On some flags, the stars were in a circle. On other flags, the stars formed a square. Stars were in rows on most flags.

The Second Flag

In 1791 and 1792, two more states became part of the United States. Lawmakers changed the flag to include these states. They added two stripes and two stars to the flag. By 1795, the flag had 15 stars and 15 stripes.

14

"The Star-Spangled Banner"

In 1812, the United States went to war with Great Britain again. The British attacked U.S. Fort McHenry. A large flag flew over Fort McHenry.

Francis Scott Key and Dr. William Beanes watched the fighting from a boat. In the morning, they looked outside. The flag was still flying over Fort McHenry. The United States had won the battle.

Francis Scott Key wrote a poem about the Fort McHenry flag. His poem was made into a song. It was called "The Star Spangled Banner."

Many Americans sang the song. They began to think of the flag as a symbol of bravery and freedom. In 1931, the song's name was officially changed to "The Star-Spangled Banner." It became the national anthem.

A New Flag

By 1818, the United States had grown to 20

states. Lawmakers met to talk about a new flag.

They decided to remove two stripes from the flag.

The 13 stripes would stand for the 13 original states.

Then five stars were added, one star for each state.

Every time a state was added, a star would be

added to the flag. Today, the flag has 50 stars.

The Pledge of Allegiance

In 1892, Francis Bellamy wrote a pledge to the flag. His words became known as the Pledge of Allegiance. The person saying the pledge promised to be loyal to the flag and to the United States.

Today, most students say the Pledge of Allegiance every morning at school. They face the flag and place their right hands over their hearts. They promise their loyalty to their country.

The Flag Code

In 1923, the National Flag Conference set up rules

for the flag. These rules included how, where, and

when to display the flag. These rules were called the

Flag Code. In 1942, President Franklin D. Roosevelt

made these rules into laws.

Flag Day

People have celebrated the flag since the late 1800s.

The country celebrates Flag Day on June 14. Every year,

the president asks Americans to proudly fly the flag.

Cities hold patriotic parades and speeches. People wear

red, white, and blue clothing. The nation honors the

flag on this day.

Symbol of a Nation

The flag has changed many times since it was designed in 1777. But, the flag's meaning has never changed. The flag stands for bravery and freedom. It makes people feel proud of their country. The flag is the most important patriotic symbol in the United States.

Fun Facts

• President William H. Taft was the first president to set exact guidelines for how the flag should look. In 1912, he said that the stars should appear in rows. Each star should have one point facing up.

• The flag that flew over Fort McHenry was 30 feet (9 m) tall and 42 feet (13 m) wide.

• One of the laws of the Flag Code is to never let the flag touch the ground.

• The U.S. flag has not changed since 1960. Hawaii became the fiftieth state in 1959. The fiftieth star was added to the flag on July 4, 1960.

• The world's largest U.S. flag is 37 feet (11 m) tall and 71 feet (22 m) long. The flag hung in the U.S. Post Office Building in Washington, D.C., in 1922.

Glossary

colony—a group of people living in a new territory but still guided or ruled by another country. Great Britain ruled the American colonies.

display—to put out to be viewed.

lawmakers—people who make laws.

loyal—to be faithful to something or someone.

national anthem—a song that has been chosen to represent a country. "The Star-Spangled Banner" is the U.S. national anthem.

patriotic—showing love for one's country.

pledge—a promise or an agreement. People who say the Pledge of Allegiance are promising to be loyal to the United States.

symbol—something that stands for something else. On the U.S. flag, a star is a symbol for a state.

31

On the Web

To learn more about the U.S. Flag, visit ABDO Publishing Company on the World Wide Web at **www.abdopublishing.com**. Web sites about the U.S. Flag are featured on our Book Links page. These links are routinely monitored and updated to provide the most current information available.

Index